ENDORSEMENTS

"*The Magic of Positivity* and its "Law and Pillars of Strength" clearly show how positivity can be a great way to live. Having known Norm for three decades now, I can tell you that he not only talks this philosophy, he lives it!"

-**Dr. Ivan Misner**, *NY Times* Bestselling Author and Founder of BNI

* * *

"Positivity is key to all that we do. The Pillars of Strength and stories shared in *The Magic of Positivity* compliment the importance of maintaining a positive attitude, regardless!"

-**Jack Canfield**, Co-Creator *Chicken Soup for the Soul*® Book Series and #1 *New York Times* Bestselling Author, *The Success Principles* (TM)

* * *

"The Magic of Positivity is simple, straightforward, and it speaks the truth. One of the great concepts taught in this book is that if you have and practice a positive attitude, you can master whatever you do in your life. Norm not only teaches and writes about this, he lives it. I highly recommend reading these words of wisdom from a true gentleman."

-**Kody Bateman**, Founder and CEO, Send Out Cards

* * *

The *'Magic of Positivity'* truly captures the essence of embracing positivity in all aspects of our life. We are fortunate to see how Norm portrays this positivity in any circumstance. Being grateful & having a positive attitude is both an art and science. We highly recommend this book to anyone who wants to practise positivity as a way of life.

-**Mac Srinivasan** - Global Markets President(CRC), BNI

-**Meena Srinivasan** - President, Scion Social

THE
MAGIC OF
POSITIVITY

THE MAGIC OF POSITIVITY

Living Positively
Remarkable Every Day

NORM DOMINGUEZ

The Magic of Positivity: Living Positively Remarkable Every Day
Copyright © 2020 by Norm Dominguez.

Disclaimer:

The author strives to be as accurate and complete as possible in the creation of this book, notwithstanding the fact that the author does not warrant or represent at any time that the contents within are accurate due to the rapidly changing nature of the Internet.

While all attempts have been made to verify information provided in this publication, the Author and the Publisher assume no responsibility and are not liable for errors, omissions, or contrary interpretation of the subject matter herein. The Author and Publisher hereby disclaim any liability, loss or damage incurred as a result of the application and utilization, whether directly or indirectly, of any information, suggestion, advice, or procedure in this book. Any perceived slights of specific persons, peoples, or organizations are unintentional.

In practical advice books, like anything else in life, there are no guarantees of income made. Readers are cautioned to rely on their own judgment about their individual circumstances to act accordingly. Readers are responsible for their own actions, choices, and results. This book is not intended for use as a source of legal, business, accounting or financial advice. All readers are advised to seek the services of competent professionals in legal, business, accounting, and finance field.

Jones Media Publishing
10645 N. Tatum Blvd. Ste. 200-166
Phoenix, AZ 85028
www.JonesMediaPublishing.com

Printed in the United States of America
Printed 2017
Revised 2020

ISBN: 978-1-948382-04-5 paperback
JMP2020.4

DEDICATION

This book is a thank you to my family and the many people who have given me encouragement since my childhood. I am blessed and filled with gratitude for what all of you have done!

CONTENTS

FOREWORD

Congratulations! If you're reading this book, it means that you've committed yourself to a life of Positivity. Before reading this book, you might not have known anything about Positivity. If you did know of it, you may not have believed in its power. Even if you did fully appreciate Positivity, you might have had moments of weakness along the way. Friend, let me tell you: we are all the same and we have all been there! This wonderful book is meant to engage and re-energize all of us in our pursuit of Positivity. It is our chance, together, to turn the page.

If you let it, this little book can change your life and the lives of those around you in a very **meaningful way**. Would you like to be a better friend? A better parent? A better leader? If you read this book thoughtfully and humbly this is not only possible, but it is certain like few things in life.

I'd like to thank Norm Dominguez for his leadership in creating this book. It's truly an honor if any words I contribute end up in the book in any way. For those who don't know Norm, he's a mentor to more people than perhaps anyone I know. The best part is I don't even think he realizes it. He's as humble, selfless, and giving as they come. And I admire him for all that he is and does.

This book is needed more than ever before. The world is awash in chaos and uncertainty. Dark clouds loom and we worry for the future of our children, our country, and our world. Media now brings pain and horror to us in a way for which our minds are simply not prepared, let alone the minds of young people. Institutions that have encouraged collaboration and compassion for decades don't seem to be functioning like they used to. And the competition for ideas is being led by those who seem intent on taking rather than giving. Has the world completely lost its mind?

As leaders, it can seem that we are tasked with so much. Perhaps too much at times. We need to provide for our families, our customers, our employees, and our communities. We're bombarded with requests, responsibilities, and of course reality. Do you sometimes get anxious about your ability to care for those who have been entrusted to you? I know I do. And if we're honest, I think we all do at times.

What we, as leaders, need is a "Renewable Reservoir" to power us through the inevitable trials and tribulations of leadership. By Reservoir, I mean a vast pool of energy from which to fuel our efforts to serve others. By Renewable, I mean a self-sustaining and ever-increasing pool of energy. In this book, you'll find just such a Renewable Reservoir. It goes by the name of Positivity. It is powerful, vast, and ever-renewing.

When have you been your **"best self"**? What are those few moments where your personal leadership has made a significant difference in someone else's life? We have all had those moments. Now, consider what made you so impactful in those moments. I'll bet that in a majority of the cases, it was Positivity. Could you increase the percentage of time when you are your best self? How would that impact those around you, and perhaps even those you may never meet?

The ideas and experiences shared in this book offer us all a chance to recommit to a specific approach to life. I believe that we're all meant to have this approach to life. Like all the important things in life, this approach costs nothing. In fact, I think that this approach to life is actually far easier than any other alternative approaches. The best part is that Positivity is infectious. It may start with you and then influence how your children see the world, how they interact with their friends, and so on. The same is true at work. I happen to lead an organization which has Positivity in its DNA. And I've seen it work miracles for customers and business partners around the world. In other words, by internalizing what you learn in this book you can change the world. Literally, could any of us have a better legacy than influencing others to adopt Positivity?

Friends, I humbly offer you this advice: Set aside the "busyness" of life for an afternoon of time alone. Grab this book along with a notebook and a pen. Before proceeding, close your eyes for five minutes and think about all that is important and meaningful to you in life. Then, turn the page and begin.

You know the rest.

Onward,

Graham Weihmiller

Chairman & CEO at **BNI**
(Business Network International)

INTRODUCTION

Positivity (POSSI)

<u>Why positivity?</u> When we hear, see, or feel positive information, it puts our attitude in a better place. Our spirits are lifted, and we accomplish more! It puts us in a healthy mindset. As I have traveled the world, the experience of being with positive people of all ages has been remarkable. Being positive comes from within; I know when I get up each and every morning I'm grateful there's no dirt on my face and I get another day to fine-tune being positive. To reinforce this journey, there is a plaque in our home that reads 'Faith makes things possible . . . not easy.' This makes positivity real and productive.

<u>What if</u> we create a simple mechanism that makes positive attitude a habit that is being practiced daily by billions in the next decade? There would be a word (POSSI) and a prompt (thumbs up) that is associated with a movement of positivity that has no ethnic, religious, cultural, or polictical boundaries, uniting the planet. This word and prompt would be a universal picture that brings together the many efforts that are being put forth to address learning needs, curing disease, improving health, delivering medical needs, etc. This word and prompt would strengthen communication around the world!

CHAPTER 1

The Law of Positivity & Pillars of Strength

THE LAW OF POSITIVITY:

When you have and practice a Positive Attitude, you will become more excellent in whatever you do. Be Positive and you will Be Happy.

Norm's Comments

Some fun and interesting thoughts on the LAW began to stir in 2012 when Keith and I began doing 10,000-mile Skype calls about one word: attitude. The calls were triggered when we met in Johannesburg, South Africa at a training event. For the better part of 15 months we would talk about its importance in life with emphasis on the positive and negative influence it has in people's lives. Thus the story begins!

We would engage in its perception and the kind of influence it has worldwide, both good and bad, as well as the role it plays in the tasks we perform. Often-times there would be a friendly, yet serious, combative spirit in our conversations. This allowed for opinions to be shared. The direction most often explored was the importance of a 'positive' attitude in all avenues of involvement.

In early 2014, Keith shared with me the formation of the Positivity Foundation in South Africa. The purpose of the foundation was to create a global movement that would ignite and engage people around the world, showing that positivity and attitude are a win-win combination. He energized me in such a way that I made a commitment to help and support the journey. We began doing weekly Skype calls, formulating strategies to support the movement. By the end of 2015 I noted,

What If we could touch and engage a billion people by the end of 2020 in our positivity movement? Within months we came up with our own word, POSSI, which is now our logo and the use of a universal gesture: '**thumbs up**'! Combined, they are the brand.

Plus, the idea surfaced that we needed a LAW! Keith began coming up with statements which we'd discuss. We did some focus group sessions (we call them Possi Circles). We would use the 'thumbs up' gesture in conversations in conjunction with the word, paying close attention to the recipient's response, which was generally a return of the gesture and a big smile. By mid-2016 we finalized the LAW, while continuing to put forth efforts that would spread a '**positive attitude**' spirit.

To support the LAW, we've added Pillars of Strength, which are being shared with you in the coming pages! ENJOY!!!!

Keith's comments

My personal mission is **"To use the unique and extensive experiences God has blessed me with over the past 72 years to be instrumental in making a positive difference in as many lives as possible."**

In updating my goals for 2013, I was miraculously given Eph3:20 (TLB) *"Now Glory be to God, who by His mighty power working within us, is able to do far more than we would ever <u>dare</u> to ask or even dream of—infinitely beyond our highest prayers, desires, thoughts or hopes."*

I was also reminded of my 1962 Youngstown, Ohio graduation motto: <u>*"Start with what you have, make the best of it, and never be satisfied."*</u>

Far more than I could ever have dreamt of or imagined happened to me in 2013!!

I had taken over a BNI Franchise for Mpumalanga, one of nine provinces in the New South Africa. I was singled out by the CEO of this incredible, huge, international referral organization to examine and explore the only subject in both BNI's core values and code of ethics. I refer to what Norm has covered above.

At the same time, I was learning another powerful and important attribute of **Being Positive**.

In April 2012, Gregory Dewar, a 46-year-old bachelor went to IHOP (International House of Prayer) in Kansas City. On the second day he was there, he had a stroke and a fit. His identity as a South African was miraculously discovered; the next morning whilst in ICU in a top hospital where a leading neurosurgeon had "felt" he must prepare a theatre for major brain surgery, Gregory had a massive brain aneurism. Over 80% of patients do not live and a large percentage of those who survive become vegetables.

There happened to be another two brain surgeons in the hospital, and with everything being ready they were able to perform a miraculous (the only word that they could come up with as an explanation) operation. After 18 months, many hundreds of thousands of dollars, and many hours of recuperation and continued prayer, Gregory moved in with his retired parents outside Nelspruit (the last thing that was on his life's plan!). In 2015 he built his own home and is now living an '**almost normal**' life. He is an exceptional example of what a **positive attitude** can help achieve and overcome. He is building a unique and very important Christian ministry.

"In April 2013, a longstanding friend and mentor of Gregory, who lives in Alabama, told Gregory that God had repeatedly told him to tell Gregory that "he was to meet a Keith." Gregory told this to his father, Billy, and a while later Billy bumped into me (Keith Dyer).

Gregory and I met the next day, and from that moment on we have known "peace beyond understanding." We are so humbled and indeed excited to KNOW that there is a **definite purpose** for all these miracles that have happened to bring us together.

Gregory played a big role (and continues to do so in the background) in contributing to Keith's journey with Norm and supporting the Possi dream as it grows and continues to materialize.

Positivity Pillars of Strength

1. **Show That You Care (STYC).** This is the most frequent display of positivity I can think of, and the simplest. It comes via an action. Before social media, which covers since the beginning of mankind, it has been a common practice that is exhibited in many ways; a hug, a word or phrase, a gesture, a look, etc. And now a text, a tweet, an email, a post, an emoji, etc. This **caring message** provides warmth, love, appreciation, affection, passion, and happiness that endures for life!

2. **Accept Responsibility (AR).** The buck stops here. This is one of the top characteristics of a great leader. It acknowledges celebration and defeat, with no ifs, ands or buts. Whether on the home front or in the workplace, the frequency of occurrence is limitless!

3. **Treat With Respect (TWR).** This pillar has no boundaries. It is not a reward, as ALL human beings deserve this form of **positive recognition**. It

is understood, some will abuse the laws of mankind and God, and they will be punished accordingly. At the top of the TWR list are family and best friends!

4. **Keep Your Word (KYW).** This pillar brings to light the often-stated expression of 'think before you speak.' There are far too many occasions when we open our mouths with words that echo a commitment we're unsure can be fulfilled. Take a deep breath, and count to three before responding to what's been said!

5. **Always Think Remarkable (ATR)** relates to being truthful whenever the question 'How are you?' is posed. The common response is fine, okay, good, etc. which can often be an untruth. By saying 'remarkable,' you have given yourself flexibility. Plus, you carry a type of uniqueness that draws a look of curiosity, even a smile!

6. **Enjoy A Little Craziness (EALC)**
provides relaxation and relief from the
pressures we face. It ignites physical and
mental juices that can be accompanied
by laughter. When this pillar is triggered,
all else is put in its proper place. There is
a **special feeling** of passion, happiness,
and positivity!

* * *

CHAPTER 2

Making Positivity a Habit

Imagine getting up every day knowing that the majority of your day is going to be **positively remarkable**. This includes having a rough night's sleep. Pretty cool, right?

When you adopt a mindset of making positivity a habit, the world becomes a better place, regardless of the distractions that may cross your path—even when there are major distractions!

February 5, 2004 - Norm Dominguez personal journal entry.

After a brief phone call with Sandi (my wife) and Tera (our daughter), and leaving a voice phone message for Ed Crane (a business associate in San Francisco) on the evening of January 12, 2004, I had a life-altering moment. It was around 5:45 PM when something I never imagined would occur: a mild stroke put me on the floor of my headquarters office in San Dimas, California. It was a message from God saying I needed to make a change.

As I sit in my kitchen in Scottsdale, Arizona, at 9:40 PM 24 days later, knowing after 35 years of adult personal and professional commitment, I have to approach my health with a kinder and gentler mindset. No longer do I have the luxury to operate a marathon lifestyle without adequate rest.

I must now set a different tone as a leader that displays the wisdom of discipline. My life has changed! I am blessed, as the Lord has given me the opportunity to step forward and show that I have listened.

Now I must rest, as there is a new day on the horizon!!

February 7, 2004 - Norm Dominguez personal journal entry.

From the moment knowledge of my stroke was released, the outpour of support has been tremendous. From family and my best friend, Jack Killough, has come personal attention and love that cannot be measured. From Ivan Misner, BNI founder, and all of our headquarters staff, I have received an ovation of prayers and wishes of wellness. I have been touched by so many within our BNI world with cards and affection. I am grateful to Steve Elliott, the backbone of my franchise operations; he hasn't missed a beat in handling day-to-day needs.

This message from God has opened my eyes. I'm blessed. I will not disappoint as I know the role I play in so many lives sets the tone for the future.

A new life, a fresh beginning. Thank you, Lord!!

The stroke was instrumental in igniting a passion to make positivity a dominant part in the lives of our global community.

To do this, I decided to adopt a plan that allowed positivity to become an everyday part of my life through what I call **TWO WORD** messaging. In this 21st century of fast-paced communications, it's important to be able to have a quick happy, healthy, passionate, and positive mechanism that allow one to put negativity in its proper place. For me, it's been the usage of many **TWO WORD** messages. I call it **My Positivity Umbrella!**

It contains six **TWO WORD** messages. They are **Be Yourself, Abundantly Grateful, Always Remarkable, Stay Calm, Reality Check** and **Intense F-A-I-T-H (Freedom-Attitude-Imagination-Trust-Hope)**. Allow me to share the meaning of each of the messages.

Be Yourself - these two words were delivered to me early in my professional life by Everett Barnhardt, a senior management executive at the Adolph Coors Company, where I began my career. They have played a key role in all of my actions personally and professionally in terms of growth. I'm so grateful!

Abundantly Grateful - as a child my parents instilled the spirit of having an attitude that was always upbeat, noting there are enough distractions. It led me to getting a great education, being an active sports participant, having a professional career that provided many leadership roles and being a family man, blessed with a loving wife, children and grandchildren.

Always Remarkable - this has to do with being truthful, a story shared in this book. It has given me lasting relationships. Life for me is indeed remarkable.

Stay Calm - often times, we are faced with situations, simple and complex. They can produce stress, discomfort, turmoil, conflict and many others feelings that may affect the well-being of one's life. By taking a deep breath and giving attention to being positive, the pressure subsides and making good decisions generally prevail.

Reality Check - this is a message that helps keep me stay in balance. I like to think I'm a **positive optimist**, knowing there are times I can be too aggressive. When this happens there are people in my life, especially my wife, that help me see what is more reasonable. This is a **good thing**.

Intense F-A-I-T-H - with this **two word** message there is a double meaning. I have a very strong attachment to spiritual guidance, yet fully respect the direction others may point themselves. At the same time, over a two-decade time frame, my professional responsibilities allowed me to travel the world. I learned a lot about the importance of freedom, attitude, imagination, trust and hope. These five words helped me to fine tune how I see life, with **lifelong learning** and leadership being key in so many ways.

Now that you've gotten a taste of **two word** messaging. In the coming chapters, as well as what you've already read, you will get a feel for the kind of impact **two words** can have. With each chapter, we'll also share some **two word** messages that you may want to adopt as you move to making positivity a habit in your life. ENJOY!!

CHAPTER 3

Show That You Care (STYC)

Jordan Adler

After recently attending an event at the Las Vegas Convention Center, I was overcome with emotion as Anthony Robbins told stories of people who reached out to their communities to make a difference. He told about a six-week trash strike in Encino, California and how a local Realtor, of his own accord and at his own expense, hired a cleanup crew to clean up all of the trash that had accumulated. In the middle of the night, while residents of the community were sleeping, his hired crews began to clean up the mess caused by the strike. The word of his good deed spread like wildfire across the community, and his real estate business exploded as a result.

Tony also told the story of a group of Chilean miners who were trapped underground for 69 days in 2010. As they awaited rescue in the collapsed mine, the story unfolded in the international news. The sunglasses brand, Oakley, decided to donate $35,000 worth of sunglasses to offer to the miners as they emerged into the bright sunlight on the day they were rescued. Oakley was praised for their act of kindness.

Upon returning from this event, I asked myself what we could do as an organization to leverage this power of kindness as well as a network of generous people to once a month impact one family or individual facing an unexpected crisis or loss. Our goal is to shower one family or individual per month with so much positivity in the form of cards and gifts that we may help to lift their spirits in a time of devastation. The movement is called The **Card Flurry** (www.cardflurry.com). This idea was inspired by Kody Bateman, entrepreneur and author from Salt Lake City, Utah. Kody has dedicated his life to bringing people together through acts of kindness.

Our first card flurry was sent to the Hunter family of Iowa who were in a tragic automobile accident just before Christmas and lost their seven-year-old daughter, Diamond, and their eight-year-old son, Donny. The magnitude of this event is inconceivable to most people and almost beyond comprehension. It's even difficult to know what to say to a family facing such a tragedy. Each of us would speak from the heart, put it in a card, and send it in an effort to ease their pain. We would show that we care. Thousands of cards and financial gifts flowed into the lives of the Hunter family as a result of this initiative.

The second card flurry was sent to six-year-old Willie Young III who, in January 2017, was shot by a drive-by shooter during a family outing. He was paralyzed from the chest down. The trauma caused to this family as a result of this horrific act is beyond words. We launched a card flurry and thousands of cards and gifts flowed into the mailbox of little Willie. To watch his **beaming smile** on the news as he thanked us for his cards and gifts let us know that we were doing the **right thing**. "Thank you for my cards and gifts everybody."

Since the launch of the card flurry, we have sent more than 4,000 cards and gifts to individuals and families in need.

"Never doubt that a small group of thoughtful, committed citizens can change the world: indeed, it's the only thing that ever has." Margaret Mead.

* * *

CHAPTER 4

Accept Responsibility (AR)

By Bonnie Moehle

Personal, Executive, and Relationship Coach

I admit it! I am a bit of a neat freak. I have been for a very long time. I like things to be neat and clean. Many years ago I had a friend who liked to **poke fun** at me. It was part of the dynamic of our relationship, and there were times when I enjoyed it and found it amusing.

However, there were also times when it would get to me and I would react. This was particularly true when he would call me a "neat freak." I would take it personally, feel attacked, and then become defensive. This particular brand of teasing really struck a chord. In addition, the more I reacted the more he would continue to poke fun at me. It got a rise out of me, and apparently he was getting something out of that.

These types of interactions would often feel uncomfortable for me; they really pushed my buttons, until I started to explore the idea of **Accepting Responsibility**. Now, at that time my understanding of accepting responsibility was to be really hard on myself. I would get so angry at myself, believing that this would somehow make me a better person. What I came to learn is that beating myself up only made me feel awful, and in addition it caused me to repeat the same behaviors and responses over and over. I didn't understand that my thoughts about myself were the underlying cause of my perceptions, behaviors, and reactions.

Eleanor Roosevelt said, "No one can make you inferior without your consent." This is the shift I began to experience when I started to **accept responsibility**. I realized that it wasn't my friend who was causing my feelings. It was my reactions to him. I had been blaming him for how I was feeling, but the blame was only causing me emotional pain. Blaming him, or anyone else, for the way I felt made me into a victim. At that time in my life, I wanted the person who I thought was the source of my pain to change so that I could feel better. Unfortunately, the likelihood of that happening was and always is pretty much zero. I was making myself reliant on another person's behavior in order to **feel happy**. The path to feeling happy cannot occur by trying to change another. The only way is through a practice of no blame—**Accepting Responsibility**.

I didn't want to feel like a victim anymore, so I began to look at the causes for my defensiveness. It was amazing how, when I truly accepted responsibility, I began to have a self-awareness, a knowing that I hadn't experienced when I was blaming. It was at this point that I had a realization. I was reacting to being called a "neat freak" because I was taking it personally. I was feeling insecure, not good enough, less than, inadequate...whatever term you like. It was then that I began to change. I began to practice self-love.

I started focusing on my strengths rather than my faults. I began to accept myself and give myself gentle, **loving kindness** rather than harsh criticisms. I made this a daily practice. This took some time, and at the beginning it felt awkward. I was so used to focusing on my faults and second-guessing myself that a positive focus felt unnatural. I kept it up. I talked to myself regularly about the essence of who I am. I paid attention to the everyday behaviors that I naturally and innately exhibit: kindness, caring, honesty, creativity, loyalty, etc. Before long, this type of thinking and this new focus became a part of how I experienced myself.

What happened next was a surprise to me. My friend called me a neat freak again, but this time my response (without any preparation or thinking) was, "Yeah, and I really like that about myself." I was taken aback. I couldn't believe the shift in my reaction. I felt great about myself. In addition, my friend stopped calling me a neat freak. Apparently, nobody keeps up a behavior unless they are getting something out of. My friend no longer got a rise out of me, and so from that point on (for the most part) he stopped giving me a hard time. By the way, we are still very close to this day.

I now know that, in both my personal life and my professional life, accepting responsibility is transformational. It is empowering. It completely shifts the way I react and respond in any given situation, which changes the dynamics in my relationships, and in the people and situations that I attract into my life. It puts me in control of the only thing I can control—my own reactions. I now see my buttons being pushed as an opportunity to accept responsibility, which gives me greater insight into the cause of my reactions. This insight helps me to heal my old response patterns so that I can be a better leader, a better friend, a better coworker, and a better partner in life. Accepting responsibility has led to a happier, more positive life, and an energy that seems to touch the lives of others as well.

Accept Responsibility is one of the Pillars of Strength necessary to Making Positivity a Habit. As I sit reflecting on my own journey, seeing life through the eyes of optimism, I am struck by the pairing of two words: **Lifelong**

Commitment. You see, the ability to Accept Responsibility and to always see opportunity in all situations takes commitment.

Life is full of challenges. We have visions of how we think people and situations should be. We have visions of the direction we think our lives should be going in, but sometimes there are obstacles—hiccups. Maybe things don't go the way we had hoped at all. However, when we are willing to make a Lifelong Commitment to Accept Responsibility with all the challenges that cross our path, we are on the road to a life of Positivity.

For me, a Lifelong Commitment to Accept Responsibility means seeing every situation as an opportunity. If things are going well, then keep moving in that direction. However, when there is a complication or a hurdle, then see it as an opportunity. How do we see challenges as opportunities? By accepting things as they are. For many, acceptance is scary. It feels like giving up or like being a doormat because most of us misunderstand the true meaning of acceptance, confusing it with resignation.

There is a vast difference between acceptance and resignation. Let's say we have a goal that we are working toward, but as we move toward it, we hit a wall. We try to push the wall, move the wall, knock the wall over, but the wall won't go anywhere. For many, this is the point where we think we are in acceptance, but we are really in resignation. We stand at the wall thinking about how we will never reach our goal and how defeated we are that there is a wall there. We call this acceptance: "Fine, I'm never going to achieve my goal. Fine, I accept that." However, this is not acceptance at all. Instead, this is the kind of thinking and energy that keeps us stuck; it is our thoughts and energy that determine our outcomes.

True acceptance requires a Lifelong Commitment to Accept Responsibility by seeing every situation as an opportunity. Now, we have a goal and as we move toward it we hit a wall. We try to push the wall, move the wall, knock the wall over, but the wall won't go anywhere. When we are in acceptance, we see the wall as an opportunity to make **new choices**. We accept that "perhaps this just isn't the way. Maybe there is a **better way**."

In acceptance, our thoughts are still focused on a positive outcome and our energy is high. This is when the light bulb goes on, we have a **great epiphany**, and it is the **perfect solution**—a way over the wall, around it, or through it. We see the opportunity.

When we make it a Lifelong Commitment to Accept Responsibility, we are no longer victims to outside forces. We see that we have the power to make new choices or change directions. We find joy in allowing the things we cannot control to be as they are, and we flow with them or around them.

And, in doing this, we make Positivity a Habit.

CHAPTER 5

Keep Your Word (KYW)

Keith Dyer

Expectations play a huge role when it comes to the phrase 'Keep Your Word' (KYW).

How often have I heard someone say, "I cannot satisfy her. I do everything I can but she is never satisfied!!"

One of the reasons I have been blessed with a happy marriage for 50 years is that my wife and I had a formal occasion very early in our marriage to have a "knee cap" session where we discussed our expectations of one another. What I thought she wanted from me was totally different from what she said she ideally expected. Knowing that her highest expectation from me is to cherish her has meant that I have not spent my life trying to figure out the impossible.

I have been able to meet—no, exceed—her expectations.

Likewise, she was way out with what she perceived to be my expectations. She was concerned that I expected a perfect cook, bottle washer, and laundry lady. Whereas the most important thing I wanted was **unwavering support**. Wow! Has she exceeded my expectations? Yes, 100-fold. She has supported me through so much, and by support I do not mean, Yes Sir, No sir, three bags full, Sir. I mean helping positively, forgiving, going along with my crazy ideas, appreciating instead of criticizing my needs, being at my side at all times, and most importantly always showing the good side of me to our daughters and others.

Expect and respect do much more than rhyme. They go hand in hand.

Take time when communicating and using words to "level the playing field" by coming to an agreement about expectations.

Keep Your Word; think before you talk. Do what you say you will do.

For a large amount of my working life I have travelled away from home for a few days (often more). On getting home I have sat down on the couch with my wife to **lovingly enquire** what she has been doing, how it has gone, etc. What she has heard coming out of my mouth is "WHAT THE HECK HAVE YOU BEEN DOING WHILE I HAVE BEEN AWAY!!" Fortunately, she knows me extremely well and takes a deep breath before she gives me her answer.

I so wish others had not reacted to what they thought I said and instead to what I know I meant.

The results and consequences of NOT Keeping Your Word are often not felt immediately. Most of the time they are intense, far-reaching, harmful, and indeed negative;

thus, very seldom positive. My fervent prayer is that this book will help you to be aware of the importance of "Keeping your Word."

We MUST hold ourselves and each other accountable to KYW.

*   *   *

CHAPTER 6

Enjoy A Little Craziness (EALC)

Four Crazy Ways to Mess up Your Mind for Long-lasting Happiness

Murali Sundaram, Happyness Coach®

Do you sometimes wonder if you'll ever be happy?

I mean **truly happy**, not just a few moments of weak sunshine in between a lifetime of cloudy gray skies.

I did. Often, my day would start out sunny, but invariably something would cloud my mood and my happiness would sink before it had even properly risen.

Think about it: You get that feeling when a driver cuts you off on your way to work, or when you have a looming deadline, or when you spill coffee on your shirt.

These stressful moments can range from something as little as an uncomfortable and annoying (even motivational) feeling, to completely debilitating depression. What's worse, these negative feelings can build on themselves very quickly until they feel out of control.

I found out one big truth about myself: I am a highly negative person!

One fine day, I decided to take charge of this enemy within me.

Maybe that's why phonetically, when you pronounce the word *'enemy'* it sounds like *'In-a-Me'*.

I made a **firm choice** to be happy in life.

I decided that I will be happy, whatever happens.

"Every decision you make or path you choose has the potential to change your life."

This is one of the craziest decisions I could ever make.

Being Happy always and for no reason is one of the craziest ideas you could ever think of.

But this idea rekindled my inner child.

I promised my inner kid that I will not lose him, come what may.

This 41-year-old is only the student; my eight-year-old self is the true happyness coach.

This awareness is the starting point of craziness in my life.

"It's not always clear when you start a path, where it may lead."

If you settle for the ordinary then you will never be able to become extraordinary.

Enjoying a little craziness is very important to live a **fulfilling life** because if you're normal then you will just be ordinary. To be special, you have to go out of the box and be unorthodox in your approach.

Are you still wondering how this craziness can help you?

A little craziness in life is a mood-elevator, highly intoxicating, powerful, productive, and likeable by many.

One who lives a slightly offbeat, crazy life, with many moments of craziness

1) is filled with loads of energy from morning to night

2) is flooded with ideas

3) channels his energy towards the achievement of those big, hairy, audacious goals

4) feels brilliant, special, perhaps even destined to change the world

5) oozes confidence, making him charismatic and persuasive.

So, whenever you are stuck in a cycle of worry, fear or over-thinking, or when your mind gets aimlessly distracted, that means it's time to **reinvent yourself**.

It's time to press the reboot button. It's time to awaken your inner child.

Hey, you are not alone. We all do.

Allow me to share with you some different crazy strategies to mess with your monkey mind to stay happy, successful, and prosperous in life.

Warning: Some of the ideas may appear crazy, so your mind may think they're very silly and discard them. Just be aware of this thought.

I do not expect you to practice all these strategies, and don't expect the same from yourself.

If something works, elevates your mood, keeps you happy, then continue the practice.

If something doesn't work, tell yourself mentally, "That's OK," and let go.

Letting go and accepting yourself as is is sometimes the best strategy for perennial happiness.

Here are my four favorite crazy practices to boost your happiness:

1) What is your vehicle's Smileage?

Let me share with you one top secret which I have been using for many years. My vehicle gives me more mileage and it increases day by day.

But I am not using petrol, diesel, or even gas. My vehicle purely runs on...

SMILES

Smileage is the key for enhanced happiness mileage.

Whenever I walk on the street, or in the nearby park, I purposefully look into those grief-struck faces and smile at them.

Do you know what they do instantly? They smile back.

Out of 20, generally 17-18 **smile back**. The other three think I'm a nut case. I don't care.

Kids smile and laugh more than adults (more than hundred times); that's why they are happier than adults.

By the way...

1. Women smile more than men.
2. Smiling releases endorphins that make us feel better.
3. We are all born with the ability to smile; it's not something we learn from others.
4. A smile is a universal expression of happiness.
5. A smiling person is thought to be more pleasant, attractive, sociable, sincere, and competent than a non-smiling person.

What can you GIVE today?

Loads of SMILES!

Such a simple act of craziness can be with you daily.

Now go and start spreading your SMILE around.

2) Power of Positive Complaining

This is my all-time favorite when my monkey starts screaming inside me, when things don't work as per the plan.

When my *"In-a-Me"* opens the Pandora's Box of complaints about why people are not kind, why people are not behaving appropriately, why people are not following rules and procedure, blah blah blah...

Voilà! I found a way to shut him down. That's called "Positive Complaining."

I immediately overrule this criminal prosecutor in my head with the power of positive complaining.

"How come every day is the happiest day?"

"Life is so perfect and constantly improving. It's not fair."

"All I need is within me now. Enough already!"

"I love everyone, everyone loves me. Humph!"

Sound ridiculous?

It's more ridiculous when we complain despite all our blessings. If we have to complain, let us complain about how good things are, or don't complain. Notice how others complain and see whether you can change those words into a positive complaint.

When this crazy habit is automatic, all is great!

Just try once today; you will love the way you start messing with your mind.

3) Crazy-Walks

Try this exercise only in your home. I have been doing this for many years and it works for me. This is a simple mindfulness exercise. You can experience it for yourself.

Every day we keep moving from one room to another within our house or our office. To add a little spice, happiness, and lightness to the situation, keep changing the way you walk between the rooms.

For example, from hall to bedroom, walk like Charlie Chaplin, walk sideways, walk backwards, etc.

Some more ways are:

- Jump and walk
- Walk on your toes
- Walk as if your left leg is shorter than the right
- Walk step by step
- Walk very slowly
- Run quickly
- Jog to the next room
- Dance and walk
- Crawl like a baby
- Walk like a 90-year-old

You can innovate many different styles of walking (depends upon how crazy you are).

This may look very silly or crazy. But this helps you to break your routines/patterns. Since you are doing something new, your mind becomes completely absorbed into that action and comes into the present moment. Your mind can't jump between past and future.

You become completely mindful. You become calm, peaceful, and happy. You feel good.

My kids laugh out loud whenever I walk like this. They start following me. The entire energy levels in the family changes instantly. Suddenly the mood in the room becomes lighter and happier.

When you are lighter, people around you become lighter. Yes, craziness is highly contagious.

4) Random Acts of Kindness(RAK)

One simple way to feel happier is to do something good for someone else. That might mean going the extra mile to help a client, being there for a friend who needs you, lending a hand to an elderly neighbor, taking care of some of the chores that your busy spouse normally handles, or writing a "thank you" note to someone who's helped you ...anything that involves a little extra kindness.

If you've been stuck in a negative mood for a while, you might find it tough to summon up the energy or motivation to do this—and you may even question whether it's worth doing at all.

Trust me, even a small gesture can make you feel much better about things (and it could mean a huge amount to the other person, too).

Some of my personal RAKs are:

1. Bring someone a cup of coffee without them asking.

2. Write a nice message on a post-it and stick it on their desk or computer.

3. Offer to help with their work. It can be your partner or colleagues, or even your neighbors.

4. Pass out candy/chocolates/cookies/fruits.

5. Leave a flower on someone's desk (anonymously).

6. Stand up and give your seat in a public transport.

7. Give way to the next guy behind you to go forward (In supermarket or airport boarding gate).

8. Give food to a homeless person and take time to talk to them.

Life is a journey comprised of small steps. The key is to take these steps every single day.

Happiness is not a mere destination. It's a journey. You can either make it miserable or make it happier. It's your choice.

Enjoying a little craziness in this journey of life provides a sense of relaxation and relief from the daily pressure of life. It helps you to kindle your physical, mental, emotional, and spiritual energies.

It keeps your mind flexible, helps you to be more compassionate with fellow human beings, fosters relationships with your partners, and blesses you with eternal hope and humility.

I was fortunate enough to read the warning signs, the signs that told me I would never be happy if I carried on thinking and acting like a compulsively busy person.

And, eventually, I learned that my happiness depended on *me* and that I could make my own blue skies.

I know you can do it, because I did.

Allow your crazy inner child to come out, right NOW, right HERE.

Just go for it!

> *"I am not asking you to change who you are;*
>
> *I am asking you to evolve into your best self."*

* * *

CHAPTER 7

Always Think Remarkable (ATR)

Norm Dominguez

This is a story about being truthful whenever the question, "How are you?" is posed. The common response is: "fine, okay, good," etc., which can often be an untruth. But saying "Remarkable," can give you flexibility, and an air of uniqueness that draws a look of curiosity, even a smile!

In November 1987, I joined a referral organization called The Network (now known as BNI – Business Network Int'l). It brings business professionals together on a weekly basis. The objective is to help them grow their business through referral marketing. The chapter of which I became a member was in Scottsdale, Arizona. At our meeting every week I'd ask our chapter president how he was and he'd say, "unbelievable", which is not the standard response you hear. After months of hearing his response, my curiosity got the best of me. I sensed there had to be something behind "unbelievable", as I found it to be a **rather unique** and positive reply. Thus, a conversation ensued!!

Our chapter president's name is Bill. I said, "Bill, tell me about this word 'unbelievable.'" "Well, Norm, I heard it at a sales training workshop I attended from Tom Hopkins as he discussed the importance of telling the truth. His (Hopkins) comments centered around the way people respond when asked how they are … and the standard response might not be totally truthful. By responding with a simple "unbelievable," one covers both sides of truth, thus addressing the whole picture of "How are you?".

My mental wheels began to spin. I thought it would be cool to have my own word that shares how I am, stating the whole truth and nothing but the truth. I did some research and came up with 'remarkable.' When I first started using the word, family, friends and others looked at me as if I was nuts. And yet its use **felt good**; I was always stating the truth, knowing that 95% of the time it was POSITIVE. The rest of the time was an internal admission of a tough moment, which we all face.

Well, it has been a serious part of my journey for many decades. Remarkable is my **life line**, along with the words of Winston Churchill: "Never, never, never give up." I believe that Life is Remarkable! Let us treat it with passion, happiness, and positivity!

* * *

CHAPTER 8

Treat With Respect (TWR): "Thank You... We Noticed!"

Andrew and Jihong Hall

Twenty-first-century China. A land alive with possibility. Home to the greatest mass migration the world has ever seen. In just 30 years, more than 400 million people have been swept from the land, inexorably drawn to the new mega cities that dominate the country today.

Cities like Shenzhen. When Deng Xiao Ping first turned his eyes here around 1980, Shenzhen was little more than a fishing village. Today, it is home to more than 10 million people, each one sucked in by an ambition shared by people around the world—the hope of a **better life** for them and their families.

Shenzhen is our home, too.

The markers of success here are everywhere you look. Cranes dominate this landscape as they have for the past thirty years, throwing ever-more stunning buildings up towards the sky. Shenzhen is a miracle of the modern age. More than 50 Chinese billionaires have built their life and success right here, and the government predicts the total GDP of Shenzhen will soon outstrip even the mighty Hong Kong just across the water.

But it is a fact of modern life that for every shining success must come countless others for whom the dream will end in the mundane. Financial betterment comes with its own cost. The young man sitting in the booth at the car park is on a twelve-hour shift. Five years ago, as he set out for Shenzhen, he had hopes and expectations, a vision that perhaps in some small way he could change the world...or at least change his world. To get here, he has made sacrifices few of us will ever have to consider. He will have left his family back in his hometown, perhaps a thousand miles away—a wife, a baby. He will see them perhaps once a year. Today, he blankly watches the barrier rise and fall, rise and fall, as cars he will never own pass him by. It is a sacrifice for family that commands respect, but too often gets none.

All of this caused my wife and I to ponder last year: what could we do? What could we do in some very small, but very personal way to show our appreciation of those we pass by every day almost without notice, but whose contribution makes our world work. To say, simply, "**Thank You**...we noticed."

Early autumn in China is dominated by the Moon Festival—a time for family and reunion. No matter how far away modern life takes you from your family, the moon festival gives a moment for reflection. A time to pause, to **look up** to the moon and know that, somewhere far off, your family is looking up, too. The Festival is celebrated with the sharing and eating of moon cakes. The cakes are round to symbolize a family joined together. An idea began to form in our minds. We would give Moon Cakes.

We decided to give Moon Cakes to all of those we pass by every day, who are the lifeblood of the city and, yet, whose work so often goes unnoticed. The street cleaner, the waiter, that car park attendant on the twelve-hour shift. And all with the simple message: "Thank you for all that you do."

Stepping out to give the first cake, we were nervous, unsure how this would work out. Would people be offended? Would they take it the wrong way? Would we be rejected? We needn't have worried. The reactions were incredible—**always surprise**, **often joy**, **sometimes tears**. A universal reaction when people realize that what they do is noticed, that they are respected, and that someone cares. And like so much in life, what you give out to others just as surely flows back to you in kind. Today, when Jihong and I ride the elevator down from our apartment, the world we step out into has changed. It is a world where it seems the sun is always shining. Where sullen faces have been replaced with glowing smiles. Where jaunty arms rise in welcome as we approach. It is a better world...a world touched by respect.

*   *   *

CHAPTER 9

Building Positivity Magic

Ready, set, here WE come! It's time to embark on an exponential Possi journey. Across this beautiful planet, we can display a positive attitude that buries chaos, uncertainty, conflict, and fear beneath an abundance of people pride. By taking little steps together, there will be a wave of excitement never seen before. This will happen as we share a united gesture, a 'thumbs up', at every turn. Toss in a wink and a smile to compliment the gesture.

You can become engaged to whatever degree of comfort you feel appropriate. If you are quiet and reserved, yet know that positivity is important in your everyday activities, performing a simple act of kindness helps advance the movement.

From the foreword by Graham Weihmiller came this request...

Friends, I humbly offer you this advice. Set aside the "busyness" of life for an afternoon of time alone. Grab this book along with a notebook and a pen. Before proceeding, close your eyes for five minutes and think about all that is important and meaningful to you in life. Then turn the page, and begin.

You know the rest.

Graham

Possi comes when we practice the Law of Positivity. **When you practice a Positive Attitude, you will become more excellent in whatever you do. Be Positive and you will Be Happy.**

It comes when all or one of the Pillars of Strength are a part of our daily routine.

We give a simple 'thumbs up' that says we believe in showing that we care, accepting responsibility, treating with respect, always thinking remarkable, keeping our word, or enjoying a little craziness.

Aristotle said, "We are what we repeatedly do. Excellence, then, is not an act, but a habit." Let us make Possi a habit!

Becoming a part of the Possi movement will support the establishment of positivity as a primary mode of communication globally. You can build a PossiPOD, share a Possi story, create a Pillar of Strength, or engage friends to display the Possi 'thumbs up' and use the magic word: 'Possi.'

A **PossiPOD** is a group of individuals who come together in support of a common positive activity. This group we like to call Podders. Each Podder is a Person Of Destiny (POD). They gather under a banner of better education, health, employment, leadership, unity between business, education and government, and more. They would meet at least quarterly and share the positive actions they are taking on the www.possiglobal.com website in the section labeled PODS.

Sharing a **Possi story** illustrates the kind of spirit that happiness, joy, hope and faith brings to all of us. You have read the stories that give meaning to The Law of Positivity and relate to each of the Pillars of Strength. We'd love to have your story by posting it on our Facebook page or on the website. Over time, we are looking to add to *The Magic of Positivity* with stories that will enhance the Possi movement. This will produce future versions of the book.

Supporting the Law are the Pillars of Strength. We welcome new Pillars. If you have an idea for a Pillar, let us know. Share it along with your story. The more Pillars we have, the stronger the Positivity movement becomes.

We believe we have a tremendous opportunity to create an atmosphere that helps each of us. We can ignite an air of happiness, joy, hope, and faith by giving each other a high-five or 'thumbs up' at every turn. This is the world of positivity!

* * *

And establish your own Positivity Umbrella with **two-word** messages that put you on a positive journey forever. We are HAPPY to include a selection of messages to claim as your own or feel free by putting your creative juices together or establish a blend of what we've shared with your own. Whatever you do, make it happen NOW.

Stay Calm	Lasting Love	Project Kindness
Express Thanks	Celebrate Now	Well Wishes
Lending Hand	Inspire Everyone	Just Smile
Thumbs Up	Find Harmony	Helping Others
Soulful Simplicity	Be Responsible	Don't Judge
Freedom First	Fully Understand	Never Fear
Show Up	Bold Move	Solid Base
Know Options	Engage Masses	Dig Deep
Listen First	Support Unity	Give Loyalty
Simply Unique	Be Genuine	Make Adjustments
Share Joy	Love Life	Boundless Energy

Happy Thoughts	Magic Carpet	Wonderfully Open
What If	Succeed Anyway	Imagine Now
Provide Balance	Think We	Always Remarkable
Fulfilling Vision	Steady Progress	Graciously Humble
Real Value	Solid Foundation	Naturally Driven
Stand Tall	Nice Response	Added Touch
Rising High	Soundly Unique	Peaceful Behavior
Extra Effort	Personal Touch	Echo Pride
Golden Silence	Think Boldly	Always Unite
Build Momentum	Show Respect	Feel Blessed
Generate Glory	Truly Awesome	Make History
Never Alone	Just Because	Clearly Fabulous
Project Warmth	Extra Effort	Everlasting Friend
Golden Result	Solid Base	Captured Treasure
Sensitive Touch	More Effort	Impeccable Character
Silent Support	Praise Results	Vibrantly Believe

Willingly Change	Act Promptly	Impressive Discipline
Classy Candor	Proudly Onward	Timeless Discovery
Right Direction	Worthy Cause	Crossing Barriers
Take Control	Eternal Promise	Managing Behavior
Fully In	Keep Dreaming	Deliver Happiness
Lovingly Hopeful	Joyous Craziness	Bright Horizon

ABOUT THE AUTHOR

Norm Dominguez is the co-founder of Possi Global, Inc. He is the Vice Chairman Emeritus of BNI, based in Charlotte, NC. For over three decades Norm was been actively engaged in the development of BNI as a global referral organization, serving in numerous leadership positions. Possi Global was created to touch and engage billions in the spirit of being positive and happy. He believes that life is remarkable! Learn more about the positivity movement at www.possiglobal.com

ABOUT *THE MAGIC OF POSITIVITY* CONTRIBUTORS

Bonnie Moehle is a personal coach, speaker, and author in the field of self-development. For over a decade, she has been actively training individuals to achieve mastery and success at work and at home. Bonnie empowers others to reach their greatest potential. She facilitates workshops nationally, and has a private practice in Phoenix. For an appointment or to order her book, *What is Happiness and Where Can I Get Some?,* call 602-717-6228 www.BonnieMoehle.com

* * *

Jordan Adler has built businesses consisting of over 200,000 distributors and nearly 500,000 customers in countries all over the globe. He's a builder, speaker, leader, trainer, and motivator. His audiences are mesmerized by his stories that inspire belief and action. Jordan sees himself as a dream-broker. He lives his personal dreams on a large scale and then inspires others to go for theirs. He is the author of the Amazon Bestseller, *Beach Money.*

* * *

Keith Dyer, a true entrepreneur, has had a few short stints in the corporate world, one being Marketing Director of a quoted company. Keith Dyer's early career was in the motor industry, pioneering specialization in the aftermarket. His passion is to have a positive effect on as many lives as possible. He specializes in promoting positive attitudes. He is the founder of the Positivity Foundation, based in South Africa, and co-founder, with Norm Dominguez, of Possi Global, Inc., promoting and growing a global positivity movement.

* * *

Jihong Hall's life story reads like an epic novel. Born in the north-west mountains of China under Mao, she drove herself to secure a rare university place—her ticket to a very different life. As a graduate in civil engineering, she was involved in early construction projects in Guangzhou and even built her first home. Keen to go further, Jihong studied English and landed in the UK in 1997, taking an MBA at the prestigious University of Warwick.

A born entrepreneur, **Andrew Hall** stepped out of Cambridge University and straight into business. In the 1990s, he ran a series of art galleries in London before discovering the business organization BNI— the cause that was to be his calling. Through the last twenty years, Andrew has helped BNI to open in the UK, Malaysia, China, Hong Kong, Macau, and Taiwan.

Andrew is the co-author of *The Handy Guide to Networking* and contributing author to the worldwide bestselling book, *Masters of Success*. A renowned public speaker, his unique style touches all who hear him, drawing invitations to speak before tens of thousands of business people around the world.

Marrying Andrew in 2003, Jihong headed back to China and today they are National Directors for BNI in China, Hong Kong, Macau, and Taiwan. They live in China with their daughter, Amara.

* * *

Murali Sandaram is an author, happiness coach, entrepreneur and trainer, as well as a keynote speaker. A Reiki Master and practitioner of Swara Yoga, Kriya Yoga, and Gnana Yoga, Murali has successfully trained more than 150,000 professionals, entrepreneurs, executives, and students on personal, managerial and leadership effectiveness, organizational development, peak performance, and wellness. He is the Director and Happiness Coach of Excel People Centric Solutions Pvt., Ltd., based in Chennai, India. He is the Executive Director of BNI, Chennai "A", and currently heading the training and leadership development of BNI India. www.happynesscoach.co.in email – murali@happinesscoach.co.in

Made in the USA
Middletown, DE
01 July 2021

43447183R00054